HOW TO HAVE
A PERFECT
CHRISTMAS

HOW TO HAVE A PERFECT CHRISTMAS

Practical and Inspirational Advice to
Simplify Your Holiday Season

Helen Isolde

A DUTTON BOOK

DUTTON
Published by the Penguin Group
Penguin Books USA Inc., 375 Hudson Street,New York, New York 10014, U.S.A.
Penguin Books Ltd, 27 Wrights Lane,London W8 5TZ, England
Penguin Books Australia Ltd, Ringwood,Victoria, Australia
Penguin Books Canada Ltd, 10 Alcorn Avenue,Toronto, Ontario, Canada M4V 3B2
Penguin Books (N.Z.) Ltd, 182–190 Wairau Road,Auckland 10, New Zealand

Penguin Books Ltd, Registered Offices:Harmondsworth, Middlesex, England

First published by Dutton, an imprint of Dutton Signet,
a division of Penguin Books USA Inc.
Distributed in Canada by McClelland & Stewart Inc.

First Printing, November, 1996
10 9 8 7 6 5 4 3 2 1

 REGISTERED TRADEMARK—MARCA REGISTRADA

LIBRARY OF CONGRESS CATALOGING-IN-PUBLICATION DATA:

Isolde, Helen.
   How to Have a Perfect Christmas: / practical and inspirational advice to simplify
your holiday season / Helen Isolde.
      p.   cm.
   Originally published: New York : H. Isolde, 1995.
   ISBN 0-525-94250-5
   1. Christmas—United States—Psychological aspects. 2. Christmas—United
States—Planning. 3. United States—Social life and customs. I. Title.
   GT4986.A1I75 1996
   394.2'663'0973—dc20   96-16171
                                                             CIP

Printed in the United States of America
Set in Bernhard Modern   Designed by Julian Hamer

Picture the perfect Christmas. Your elegant home is decorated with garlands of evergreen and holly. Your happy family is gathered around the glittering tree. Gaily wrapped gifts are piled up everywhere. The seasoned aroma of Christmas dinner streams from the kitchen, while outside snow falls softly and the sounds of Christmas carols and sleigh bells fill the air. This is a fantasy.

Now, wake up, open your eyes, and welcome to reality. Your guests are late for dinner and the roast is charred beyond an arson investigator's recognition.

Your family members are faint with hunger. The kids are fighting like trolls and you can't even threaten them with Santa because they opened their presents hours ago. Your cat takes a flying leap at a strand of tinsel and topples the tree. Grandma startles awake and spills her blackberry brandy on your carpet. Helpless, hopeless, and exhausted, you teeter on the brink of insanity.

In spite of years of experience, and more than enough intelligence to know better, most of us still hold dear some version of the perfect Christmas deep in our hearts. It is a vision made up of childhood memories, high hopes, and unrealistic expectations. But we always believe we can make it happen if only we try hard enough. The fact is, we try too hard. We try to create and live a fantasy. We try to make it perfect, and instead Christmas becomes an annual crazy-making event. The harder we work at making Christmas perfect, the more likely we are to fall flat on our weary faces. Perfection is not possible. It is not a part of the human condition, nor is it even a definable goal. Real life is not choreographed, it is chaotic. Accepting that, we can learn to love it.

This book is my Christmas gift to you and to anyone who has ever struggled to make Christmas perfect. It is a collection of hard-learned lessons from many years of Christmas experience, some good advice from some good friends, and a little bit of whimsy. It grew from the realization that there are some few things in life that we can control but many more that we can't, some things that we can change, and lots that won't be the least bit different in our lifetime, or the next.

Some of these sayings are funny, some are serious; some offer advice that is easy to take, some speak to goals that are ideals. Taken together, they suggest that we look closely at what we are trying to do compared to what we are doing. You are a very important part of everyone's Merry Christmas. Relax and enjoy. The greatest gift we have to offer each other is ourselves: rested, cheerful, and ready to spend a perfectly happy holiday together.

Have a perfectly Merry Christmas!

Accept the fact that holidays,
like people, are not perfect.

Remember, happiness is wanting
what you have,
not having what you want.

Check the batteries
in your camera
and buy lots of film.

Contemplate the unique symmetry
of a single snowflake.

Plan the Christmas menu
knowing that the cook
deserves a holiday too.

Appreciate the fact that
the cold outside makes
you feel warm inside.

"Some Assembly Required"
does not mean you
can put it together on Christmas Eve.

Listen well to someone
who's feeling disappointed.

Remember, you get
another chance next year.

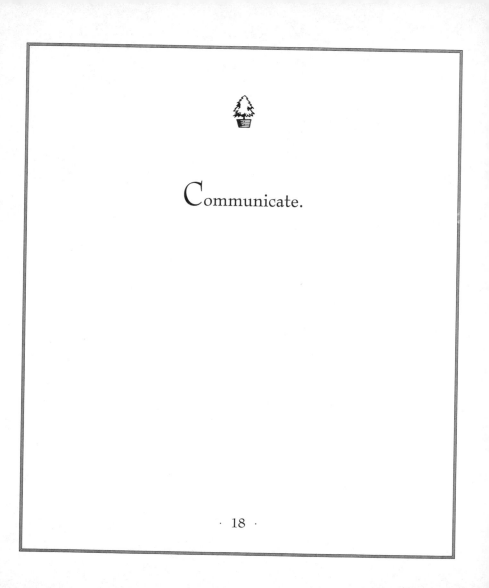

Communicate.

Remember, holiday cheer
does not come in a bottle.

While shopping, pretend
you are walking for exercise.

Think about someone
who is trying to think
of the perfect gift for you.

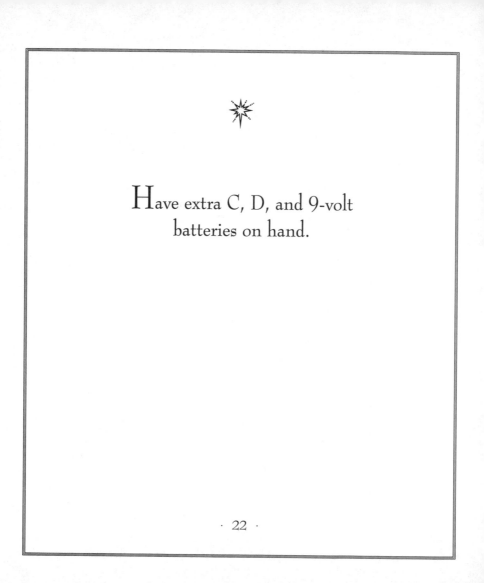

Have extra C, D, and 9-volt
batteries on hand.

Assess your expectations
of yourself and others.
Then, lower them.

Live every moment
and cherish it.

Understand that only you
can make yourself less busy.

Spend an evening recalling
your favorite holiday memories.

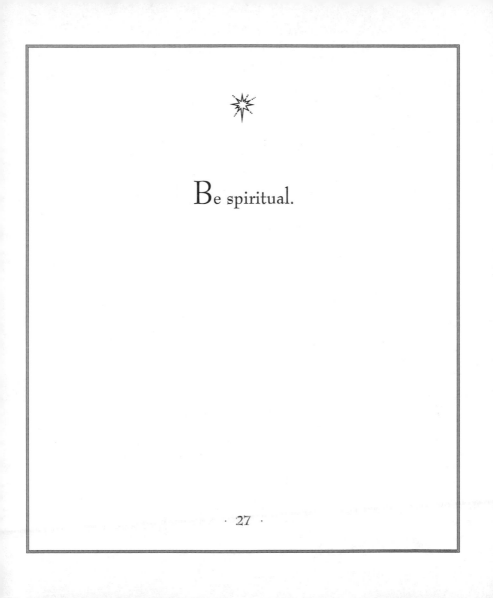

Be spiritual.

Allow yourself to grieve
for people who are no longer here.

Cut your social calendar in half.

Burn candles.

See the angels among us.

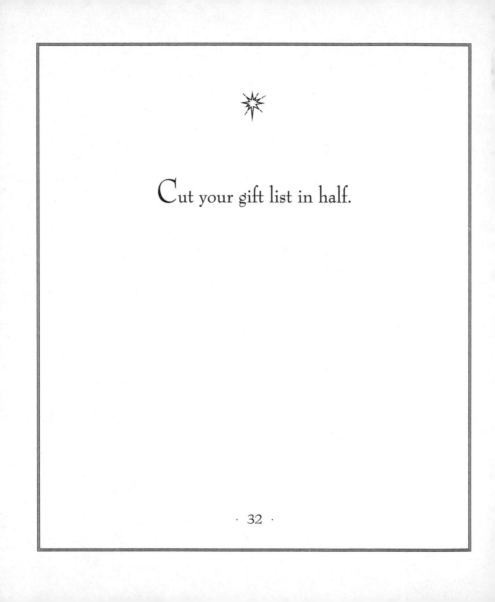

Cut your gift list in half.

If one store is out of something,
resolve not to look
for that item elsewhere.

Bake cookies only as long
as you enjoy the process.

Don't give anyone fruitcake
unless you know they love it.

Resolve to set time aside
for yourself.

Seek rest.

Eliminate the word "should"
from what
you expect of yourself
and others.

Believing you can do it all
is setting yourself up
for disappointment.

Don't expect to have
the perfect gift for everyone.
You won't, nor will they.

Ask someone else
how they are coping.
Listen to what they say.

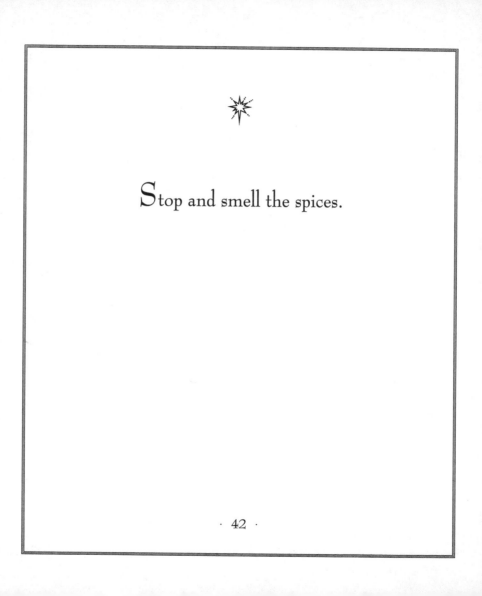

Stop and smell the spices.

Don't fight for close-in parking.
Instead,
enjoy walking in the fresh air.

Wrap no more than
five presents at a time.

Ponder genuine joy.

Recognize that perfection
is a direction, not a goal.

Smile anyway.

Ring bells.

Try to recall
the magic of childhood.

Consider a fake tree.

Learn to let go
of little resentments.

Stir cocoa with candy canes.

Tolerate pretension
but don't practice it.

Use real satin ribbon
and save it for next year.

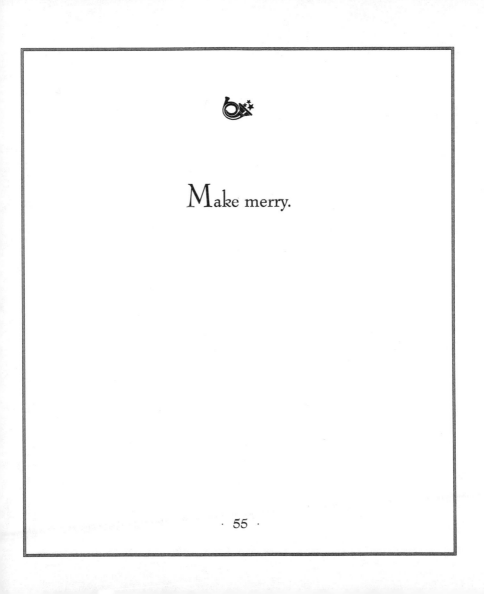

Make merry.

Focus inward when alone,
outward when with others.

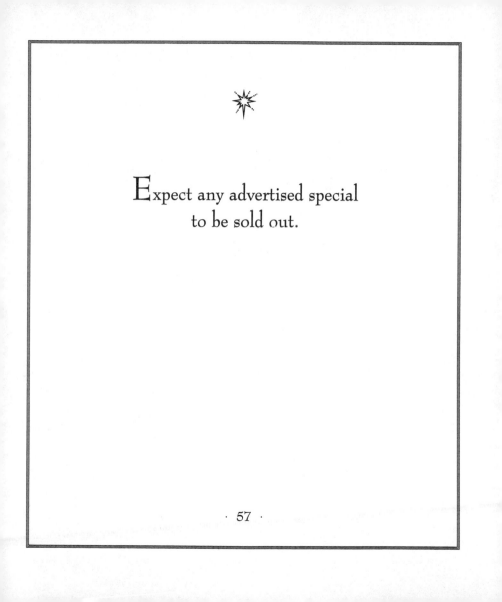

Expect any advertised special
to be sold out.

Understand that alcohol
is worse than ice
on the highway.

Check with stores
for expanded hours and shop
only in the very early
and very late ones.

Give of yourself.
But don't give up your self.

Save at least three evenings
a week to write cards
and wrap gifts.

Make snow angels.

Don't shop for friends
on your lunch hour.
Go to lunch with your friends.

Adopt a larger perspective.

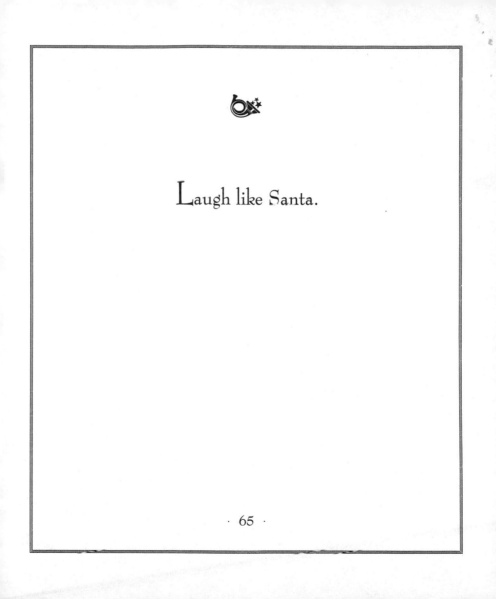

Laugh like Santa.

Sympathize with a store clerk.

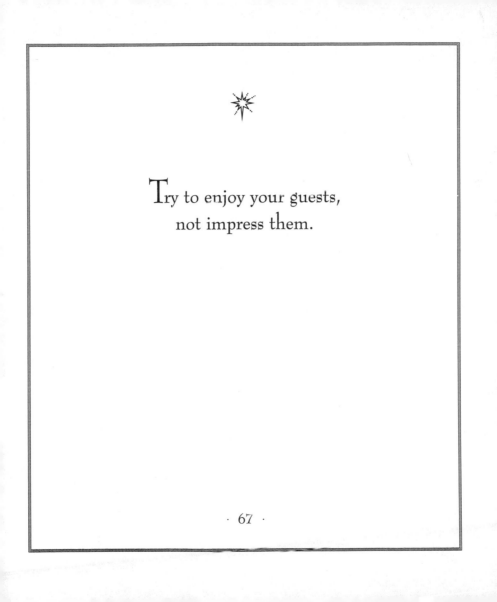

Try to enjoy your guests,
not impress them.

Remember that ads
are created to create desire.

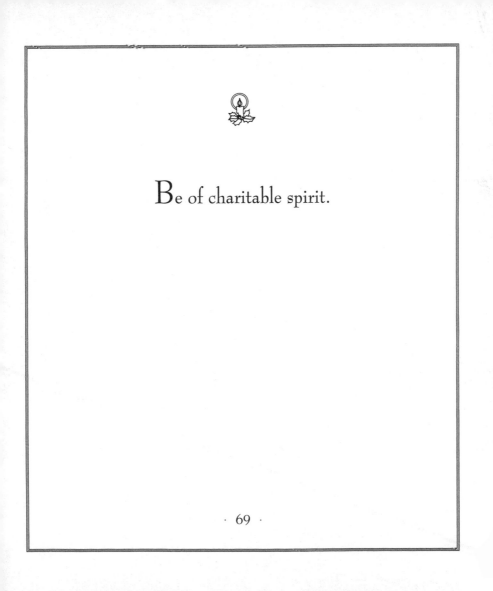

Be of charitable spirit.

Compliment every
fifth person you see.

Telephone someone
you haven't spoken to
all year.

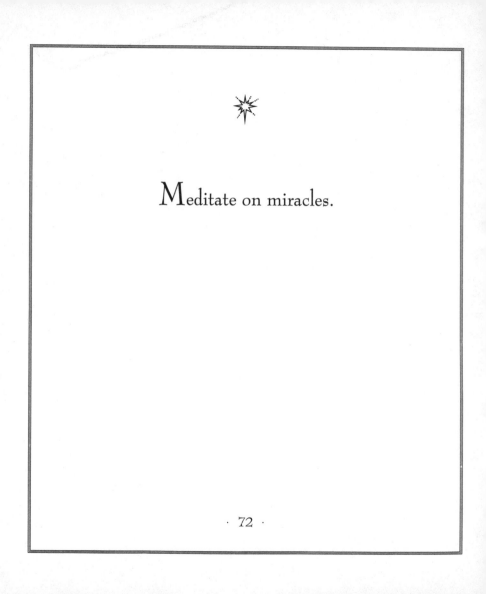

Meditate on miracles.

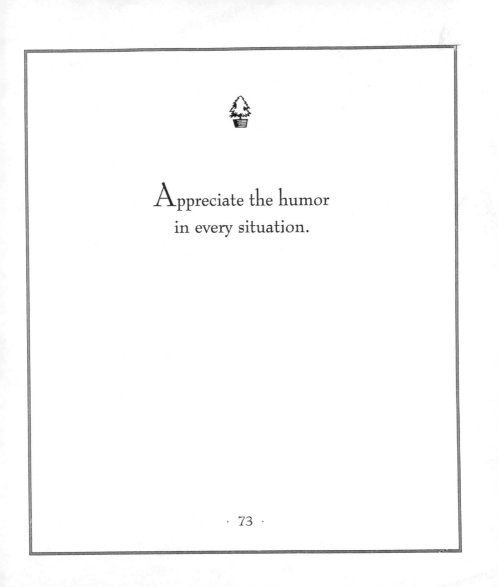

Appreciate the humor
in every situation.

Realize that the dinner
will not be ready on time,
nor will the guests.

Promise yourself
one good laugh a day.

In a crowded store,
notice something nice
about each person in line.

Resist the urge
to make a gingerbread house.

Remember, striving too hard
for perfection
precludes reaching it.

Know that material gifts
are not the measure of friendship,
nor can they create love.

Think about the beauty
of your tree before it is trimmed
and make sure you have
a good tree stand.

Know that good friends
are better than big packages.

Have plenty of
package wrapping,
video, and audio
tape on hand.

Practice hugging.

If someone has everything,
make a charitable donation
in their name but don't
give out their address.

Think about your three best
accomplishments this year.

Relax and enjoy,
you've done
everything you can.

Sing Christmas music every day.

Take notes for next year.

Wear flannel.

Ask for help in the kitchen.

Food is good.
Too much food is not good.

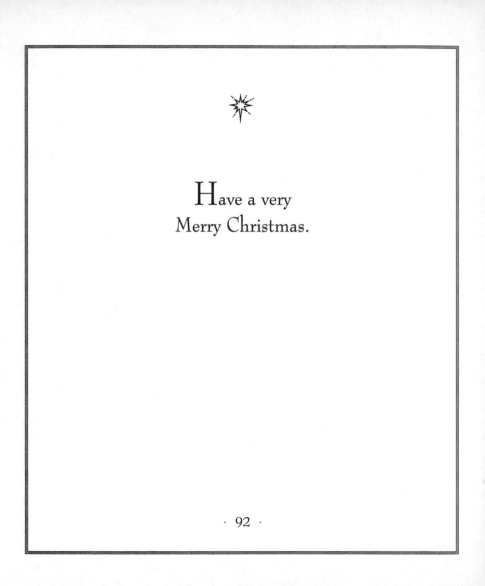

Have a very
Merry Christmas.